INDELIBLE

INDELIBLE

Don Thompson

Clare Songbirds
Publishing House

Clare Songbirds Publishing House Poetry Series
ISBN 978-1-957221-33-5
Clare Songbirds Publishing House
Indelible© 2025 Don Thompson

Printed in the United States of America
FIRST EDITION

140 Cottage Street
Auburn, New York 13021
www.claresongbirdspub.com

The author wishes to thank the publications in which the following poems first appeared.

Adelaide: "Vespers Update", "January 31st", "Sunday Afternoon"

Ariel Chart: "Snow on the Hills"

Courtship of the Winds: "Bad Afternoon"

Foxglove: "Hush"

Jalmurra: "Fallow (1)", "Fallow (2)"

Literary Yard: "Earthquake Weather"

Medusa's Kitchen: "Stasis"

Off Course: "Indelible"

Pangolin Review: "Some Toads"

Red Eft : "Test"

Right Hand Clapping: "Crow"

Shot Glass Journal: "Yellow"

Contents

Indelible

Not much remains of the lamb,
though not long dead:
only unbleached-so-far
bones and
a sheet of vellum.

You wonder what you'd
write on it
that would matter
and what sort of ink
would hold up for how long.

Vespers Update

In this season, the sun sets
like an afterthought, its light
already non-luminous.

The hills mostly murk
with some leftover mauve
that's gone flat.

But Venus burns a hole
in the West, intense
and more adamant than ever.

Fallow (1)

Sunlight so thin and so dry
it crumbles, settling like dust.

Without water, roots
have learned how to live on illusions.

No scrub grows above knee-high,
spindly and infirm—

and a green of some sort
you'll soon have to call gray.

Crow

A hangdog crow, indecisively
slumped on a post,
hesitates between nowheres.

Something's crushed his gusto.

Failure must be inherent
in his life too. Sometimes
feathers get their sheen
from a slow leak of serotonin.

Bad Afternoon

The sky's too low and solid,
a failed shade of bluish
plaster. Clouds
scrape their backs against it,
but keep drifting.

Everything else holds still
as if, like us,
always thinking too much—
not sure what to do next.

Trees wait for the wind
to move them, unmoved.

Finally one crow, fed up,
swats at the thick air
and shoves its way out of sight.

Snow on the Hills

The scant snow's an afterthought,
no more: the storm
at midnight impatient
to shrug off this place
and reach higher ground.

Still it blesses us briefly
at sunrise—a vermilion gauze
of light, shimmering
with the urgency of all things
never meant to last.

January 31st

1.
The sun through an
oily pond water smear
of its own light,
almost too dim to see by.

2.
Winter but not cold
enough to convince—
stagnant air only
a few degrees below tepid.

3.
Icebound up north,
tropics stunned by heat:
we're neither nor,
lackluster, in-between.

Stasis

Ditch water down on its luck
and stagnant, stays put...

Nothing's going anywhere.

No clouds in the slate sky
deceive you with
their illusions of long journeys.

A slow swirl of birds
flutters like handkerchiefs
waving goodbye—

a meaningless but unbroken
tradition among them.

Some Toads

Infamously ugly, some toads
seldom hop, but
with the long, slow steps
of a stalker,
creep into and out of dank places.

Their color's awful—a goulash
of greens, browns and black
that's no color at all
and splattered with warts.
Your skin crawls.

And yet, contra naturam,
you take delight
in their outsiders' night music—
that high tenor, a bit sharp,
but irrepressible.

Test

He looks up, nitric eyes
testing you like acid on gold.
You feel fake. Exposed.

For once the crow has no comment,
which says it all,
and shrugs himself into the air

like a pawnbroker turning his back,
offering nothing—not a cent
for your most precious heirloom.

Alive

No one remembers this tree's name
or admits willingly

that its roots go any deeper
into hard ground than varmints dig.

Ash gray bark, scabrous,
with branches dry enough to burn—

if you want a pitiful little fire
crackling like insects in a zapper.

And yet, it's alive, showing off
a fistful of new leaves—green,

though not a green you'd ever paint
any room you live in.

Yellow

Nothing grows near greasewood
with its tar pot odor
and thirst
that sucks up every drop.

So the shrub stands alone in gravel
rising from its own bones
in tatters—as sordid
as the undead.

Nevertheless you willingly hold your breath
to pause and admire
its shaggy yellow flowers—
shriveled in the heat, perhaps,
but perennial.

Earthquake Weather

The air's gone underground
into legendary deep caverns
locals believe in.

And a river down there
broods in the dark—inexhaustible
aquifer of silence.

Hot and dry and still.
We look at each other
without saying what we know.

Fallow (2)

The last crop to suffer on this field
had be be plowed under.

No water—
or none that anyone could afford.

Russian thistle has a lease now,
until the wind evicts it.

A hawk circling overhead
gives up and drifts away hungry…

This place makes you think about
what it means to be fallow.

And how closer than that hawk is,
the Aqueduct rushes south

overflowing with, so it seems,
all the water there is.

Sunday Afternoon

Cumulus out of Constable
loiter to the north,
left behind by a storm.

Calm now.

Pools of rainwater
like cloudscapes
abandoned, unfinished,
by weekend artists
who had to get back to work.

Hush

The night, this night anyway,
has requested quiet.

The owl complies, sounds one note
pianissimo on a marimba
with a soft mallet.

No crickets fidget.

No feral tom cats talk trash.

Even the hound over on the next farm
howls for only a few minutes
and then, whatever had been bothering him,
lets it drop
and drifts off to sleep.

Don Thompson has been writing about the San Joaquin Valley for over fifty years, including two dozen or so books and chapbooks. He is a past winner of the Sunken Garden Prize and the Eric Hoffer Award. His most recent publication is *The Eightieth Year* (Wipf and Stock).